SOWING THE SEEDS

Roots of Youth Ministry Series

This series addresses ecumenical and uniquely Presbyterian youth ministry concerns. Volumes in this series are intended for both professional and lay adults engaged in youth ministry.

Series Writers
Rodger Nishioka
Bob Tuttle
Lynn Turnage

Series Editor
Faye Burdick

Titles In Series
The Roots of Who We Are
Surveying the Land
Dealing with Crisis
Rooted in Love
Sowing the Seeds
Growing Leaders
Growing a Group

SOWING THE SEEDS

RODGER NISHIOKA

Bridge Resources
Louisville, Kentucky

Edited by Faye Burdick
Book interior and cover design by Pamela Ullman

First edition

Published by Bridge Resources
Louisville, Kentucky

Web site address: http://www.bridgeresources.org

PRINTED IN THE UNITED STATES OF AMERICA

98 99 00 01 02 03 04 05 06 07 — 10 9 8 7 6 5 4 3 2 1

Library of Congress Cataloging-in-Publication Data
Nishioka, Rodger Y.
   Sowing the seeds / Rodger Nishioka.
      p.   cm. — (Roots of youth ministry series)
   ISBN 1-57895-013-9
   1. Christian education of young people. I. Title.   II. Series.
BV1485.N57 1998
268'.433—dc21   98-6760

In memory of Bob Ames (1964–1995), who sowed seeds of faith and joy wherever he went, and with a grateful heart to the courageous and loving people of the White Memorial Presbyterian Church in Raleigh, North Carolina, who cared for Bob and his family during his illness.

Contents

Introduction

My mother's parents were farmers. They possessed the wondrous ability to transform a plot of land into rows of fresh vegetables and vibrant flowers bursting with color. On visits to their home in Hayward, California, their four grandsons would enjoy playing on the land behind their home. I can still remember watching my grandfather Tamura go through his daily routine of watering and picking at weeds here and there. I can remember, too, my grandmother Tamura heading out to the rows of corn to bring in fresh corn for dinner. It's an amazing thing to sow seeds into the ground and then to reap the harvest of what you have sown.

This book is titled *Sowing the Seeds* because its focus is on how we as faithful youth ministry leaders might help sow seeds of faith in the young people entrusted to our care. We begin with a look at how we can help nurture the faith in young people through understanding John Westerhoff's faith styles. We move next to a study of the youth culture today and its implications for our ministry with young people. What follows is a critique of the church school, a place where traditionally we have been sowing the seeds of faith. Next, helps are provided for those persons facing challenges in managing the behavior of young people in the classroom or youth group. Finally, we focus on the particular task of sowing the seeds of faith with young people in small-membership congregations.

Acknowledgments

I continue to be grateful to my colleagues, Lynn Turnage and Bob Tuttle, for their friendship and partnership in writing this series. We are all indebted to our fine editor, Faye Burdick, who envisioned this series. Lynn Turnage, Bob Tuttle, and I are especially grateful for the gracious hospitality of Flora and Rick Hobson and their sons David, Pat, and Cauley for the generous use of their lake house in the writing of this series. Finally, I am so grateful for my community of friends at McCormick Theological Seminary in Chicago, who have provided me with both nurture and challenge. Special thanks to Julia Carson, Eileen Parfrey, and Chris Stewart for teaching me so much about faith and faithfulness.

1
On Sowing the Seeds

It was one of those times in youth ministry when you are gifted with an "epiphany moment" by the Holy Spirit. It was an "Aha!" so great you couldn't miss it. I was with my youth group, and Halloween was approaching. The team of youth and adult leaders who planned that particular session went all out on the Halloween theme. We had a great time doing all kinds of Halloween-related activities, everything from carving pumpkins to singing pumpkin carols. At the end of the evening as we were gathering up our Halloween goodies to take home, Kyle, one of the young people, turned to me and said, "You know, this was fun and all, but what does this have to do with my faith?" As is often the case with epiphany moments, I was unprepared for the question. Kyle and I talked more. He understood the idea of being in community and our belief that community is the body of Christ. He understood that we had spent the evening doing community building or, if you will, body building. But for Kyle and many others like him, this wasn't enough. At a young fourteen, he was still very much a concrete thinker. Kyle needed concrete, explicit connections. "I don't mean we have to be serious all the time," he said later. "But I just think we should deal with faith stuff. I mean, isn't that why we're here, anyway?"

Kyle was right. This is why we are together. Community building is crucial to our life together, but we are not building community for community's sake. We are building community to strengthen the body of Christ so that in faith we might transform the world. Certainly faith is a gift of God. As leaders in youth ministry, we can no more help young people get faith than we can save them through our own doing. We trust in God for the giving of faith and the grace of salvation. But we know that we can create environments where faith can be nurtured.

In the Gospels of Mark, Matthew, and Luke, Jesus is recorded as telling the same parable about faith:

Listen! A sower went out to sow. And as he sowed, some seed fell on the path, and the birds came and ate it up. Other seed fell on rocky ground, where it did not have much soil, and it sprang up quickly, since it had no depth of soil. And when the sun rose, it was scorched; and since it had no root, it withered away. Other seed fell among thorns, and the thorns grew up and choked it, and it yielded no grain. Other seed fell into good soil and brought forth grain, growing up and increasing and yielding thirty and sixty and a hundredfold. And he said, "Let anyone with ears to hear listen!" (Mark 4:3–9)

Jesus later goes on to explain to his disciples that the seed is the word and God is the sower. The challenge for the believer is to be good soil so that when the seed of the word is planted in us, we might bear fruit for God. Clearly, this is the work of youth ministry. Our task is to help our young people be good soil. To be sure, community building is an important part of that. But Kyle opened my eyes to the reality that we must be aware of where our young people are in their faith development. For some, the implicit references to faith and belief are enough. For others, like Kyle, they mean little. For Kyle to be good soil, he needs to be confronted squarely with talk and images of faith and believing.

Westerhoff's Faith Styles

Several years ago, John H. Westerhoff, while teaching at Duke Divinity School, published a book titled *Will Our Children Have Faith?* In it, he outlined four faith "styles." Westerhoff was careful not to call these faith styles "stages" for fear that they might be taken as a linear progression, stepping from one to the other and never returning. Instead, he called them styles and compared them to the rings of a tree's growth. When you slice through the trunk of a tree and examine it, there are distinct rings indicating different moments in the tree's growth. Westerhoff compared our life of faith with the rings of a tree and noted that an older tree would have more rings than a younger one. His premise is that we may travel through these different styles over and over again based on our life experiences and God's presence with us.

Experienced Faith Style

The experienced faith is the only style to which Westerhoff assigns an age. He says that for many believers this experienced faith happens in early childhood. In this faith style, our faith is gained through experiences around us. When we hold hands at the dinner table and say a prayer about God being great and good, we may not fully understand what we are saying, but our experience is helping our faith and helping us grow. Going to church school, reciting verses, singing songs, taking part in the Christmas pageant, and placing a coin in the offering plate are experiences that help prepare the good soil to receive the faith that the Holy Spirit gives. When you ask a group of youth or adults who have participated in church since their childhood to recite for you their "earliest childhood church memory," you are hearing evidence of the experienced faith style. At an early age, these people experienced faith in a real way, and it has stuck with them.

Even young people and adults who are completely new to the faith live through this experienced faith style, although far more rapidly than children who are nurtured in Christian homes all their lives. Dan joined my father's congregation at age sixteen. He had no church background but felt compelled to come to worship one Sunday. Since he was in my high school church school class, I and the other co-teacher began tutoring Dan on the side about the practices of our faith (the Lord's Prayer, the Apostles' Creed, etc.). Worshiping with Dan was a treat. He was alert to everything that we did and asked many questions (most of which I couldn't answer!). While he was also in an affiliative and even searching faith style (you'll see these in a moment), every new experience in our congregation was also a part of his experienced faith style. But Dan didn't stay long in this faith style. He began right away to articulate a sense of belonging, showing signs of his growing into the affiliative faith style.

Affiliative Faith Style
Westerhoff characterizes the affiliative faith style in three ways: yearning to belong, focusing on feelings, and seeking authority.

Belonging
One part of the affiliative faith style is the yearning to belong—to be a part of something. When young people are in this style, they are needing to feel a part of a group. They very much want to be needed and accepted for who they are. Persons who are in this faith style will care less about what is being preached or taught or said and will care more about what is being done to include them and help them feel welcome.

This faith style is common among young people, especially early adolescents who are often consumed by whether or not they belong and what others think of them. David Elkind, in his book *All Grown Up* and No Place to Go, calls this the "imaginary audience syndrome," where young people constantly imagine that no matter where they go, they are the center of attention. I've talked with Elkind and have told him that I don't always believe this is imaginary. Young people *do* watch other young people all the time. They notice what they wear and how they wear it, how they stand or walk or talk or dance or you name it. In the midst of the insecurities that loom so large at this age, the need to affiliate with a group and to feel like you belong is an enormous one. In Westerhoff's faith development theory, the yearning to belong to faith in some way can only be manifested through a faith community.

I remember growing weary of Beth. Perky and excitable, Beth was constantly seeking to please everyone and always checking her place in the group. Her need to be liked was overwhelming at times. At my first reading, I simply placed her as one of the more "needy" in the group, but after reading through Westerhoff's faith development theory, I better understood that Beth simply needed to be assured of her belonging to the group. After a while, I began to say directly to her, "You know, Beth, you belong here and nothing you can do will change that." She looked at me quizzically at first, but she could tell I meant it. Eventually, her need to belong decreased, and I could see she was growing into another faith style.

Affections (Heart)

Another part of the affiliative faith style is the opportunity to focus on feelings. Often persons who are in this faith style are yearning for some connection of the heart to their faith. They look to be moved and to be changed not through some new thinking but through some feeling. Several years ago I crossed paths with a young woman whom I had met at another conference. She told me how much attending that particular conference had meant to her faith. When I asked her how it had impacted her faith, she said it had "opened her heart to God." That particular conference had been filled with wonderful music, liturgical dance, banners, and many other powerful images. She clearly was in the affections portion of this faith style. Words like *awe, wonder, splendor,* and *mystery* are often used by persons in this faith style.

Authority

A final subheading in Westerhoff's affiliative faith style describes persons who are in search of authority and their faith. They are not so much looking for outside sources of authority as they are seeking ways to put their own story together with the story of their faith community and the story of faith they understand from Scripture. Often people in this faith style are trying to establish identity and tradition for themselves and for others. One summer at our national youth conference center in Montreat, North Carolina, I was introduced to a young man who had just started playing the bagpipes. He asked if he could lead the closing activity of surrounding the lake at the conference center by playing "Amazing Grace." I checked with other worship leaders, and they said it was fine. He did so and it was very meaningful. The next year he came back, and on the closing night he came up to me with his bagpipes and asked where he should start. When I told him I had to check with the new leadership to see if he could play, he was incredulous. "But I have to play," he said. "This is a tradition." It amused me that after just one time, this had become a tradition for him, and likely for a number of others. Such is the thinking of young people and adults who are seeking authority. They are desperately trying to see how their own personal story fits in with the broader story of the community and the story of our faith found in the Bible.

Searching Faith Style

Like the affiliative faith style, Westerhoff characterizes the searching faith style in three ways: doubt/critical judgment, experimentation, and commitment to persons/causes.

Doubt/Critical Judgment

One of the most challenging of the faith styles, the doubt/critical judgment form of the searching faith style is characterized by a rejection of the affiliative and can often be painful and threatening, especially to parents and stepparents and other adult leaders. Not every adolescent goes through this faith style, but many do. It's often expressed through criticism and skepticism. As young people realize the world is not cut and dry but, instead, ambiguous, they apply this same pressure to their faith and faith community. What once was taken as simple truth is now up for criticism and judgment. Troubling questions emerge. Why are there two stories of the creation account? Where did Cain's wife come from? If the flood truly happened, why is there no scientific evidence of it? Where did the dinosaurs come from? How do you account for the evolution of species? If God made all things, did God create evil, too? Why do good people have to suffer? Why does God stand by when so many people are killed or die?

These questions by their nature are critical, and because they raise doubts about the fabric of our faith, they are threatening. The important thing Westerhoff reminds us is that this is simply one of the various faith styles that we encounter in our journey of faith—a journey to which each of us is called by Christ and led by the Holy Spirit.

Experimentation

Another of the more challenging forms of the searching faith style, experimentation, means exactly what it says. There comes a time in the lives of many young people, young adults, and adults when they are led to experiment with other faiths and faith communities. In this faith style, the search takes on more meaning as individuals literally try out other expressions of faith. The search can be far-ranging. Its ultimate goal is to test the tradition in which the person has been nurtured to see how it stands up against other traditions. For many young adults, this time of experimentation coincides with new freedoms, including a departure from home, life at college or university, or a move to a new community for a new job. Like the previous searching behavior characterized by criticism and doubt, Westerhoff assures us that this is an important component in the journey of faith.

Commitment to Persons/Causes

The third and final form of the searching faith style is the commitment to persons and/or causes. In the process of searching, individuals may become attracted to particular leaders or causes and find themselves ready to give their lives away. Often, however, they do not think through the consequences of such an important decision, or they make a commitment on the basis of erroneous assumptions or fleeting emotions. This may give the appearance that the one making the commitments is fickle. Still, Westerhoff says the key issue here is one of personal power and the ability to make decisions about one's life and priorities. The nature of searching, too, is a seeking for meaning and an answer to the question What difference does it make that I exist? By committing to persons and to causes, individuals are seeking to make a difference, whether it means following a personality who has extraordinary charisma and charm or committing to a particular cause to help the poor and homeless. This idea of making a difference in the world is crucial.

Owned Faith Style

Westerhoff's final faith style is an "owned faith style." In using the term *owned*, Westerhoff says that individuals truly have reached a point where they claim their faith and faith community as belonging to them. Typical of the owned faith style is faith put into action. Beyond easy rhetoric, an owned faith is integrated into every part of a person's life. Often an owned faith comes after a major conversion experience that leads to major change in the person's life. Any profound internal conflicts have been eliminated or discounted so that the person feels a real sense of peace about his or her life and faith. Sometimes, this owned faith comes at the expense of the community of nurture.

Jed recently returned from one year of service as a young adult volunteer in the Philippines. While there, his faith was profoundly transformed. When he returned to his home congregation, he found a group of people he loved dearly who had nurtured him and supported him for many years, but he grew frustrated trying to expand their worldview and explain what a dramatic conversion experience he had encountered. "They kept treating me as if I were the same kid from vacation Bible school," Jed told me. "But I wasn't. I kept trying to explain to them how I had experienced Christ in a new way, but they weren't able to even listen to me." Sadly and to his parents' dismay, Jed has begun worshiping with another congregation.

Persons with an owned faith also find themselves seeking authentic opportunities to witness to their faith. This does not mean these people join evangelistic crusades, although they might. It often means that their faith is so much a part of who they are that without being oppressive or insensitive, they are readily able to share their faith with others. People with an owned faith have been through affiliative and searching struggles and are often able to relate their stories with those who are in the midst of those struggles.

So How Does This Work?

It's important to remember again that Westerhoff did not intend to present a linear model with a beginning and an ending but rather a model of faith styles that moves outward in concentric circles. For Westerhoff, the beginning circle is the experienced faith style. The next circle is an affiliative faith style (any one or two or all of the three forms). From there the next circle may be searching or owned, and from there, experienced or affiliative. This kind of flow represents well the journey of faith. When we reach a place where we possess an owned faith, some event inevitably throws us back to a searching faith style focusing on doubt and critical judgment. Out of that searching, we may seek an affiliative faith style focusing on authority, and eventually, all through the leading of the Holy Spirit, we end up at a place of owned faith again.

Why Is Faith Development Theory Important in Youth Ministry?

Not one of the young people or adults in your group is in the exact same place as another. And while no one fits perfectly into any of these faith styles, being familiar with them will help you know how to respond to the questions that will arise. When you feel like the core of your faith is being attacked by a young person, take a breath and know that the Holy Spirit is leading him or her through the searching faith style of doubt and critical judgment. When you are excited by a young person's willingness to do something, often anything, that puts faith into action, know that the Holy Spirit is leading that young person through the affiliative faith style to commit to persons and causes. Remember though, that these styles are meant to be *descriptive* rather than *prescriptive*. Let these styles *describe* where youth and adults are and not *prescribe* how you look at them and respond to them. As an example, let's look at several young people I've encountered in my journey. As you read about them, determine which faith style they're in and why, and then imagine your best and worst response.

Applying Westerhoff's Faith Styles— Eight Young People

1. Jamal says the world is cut and dried. He knows what is right and what is wrong. In his world, if you're Christian, you had better act like it or you're going to hell. If you're not a Christian, you're certainly going to hell. His response when confronted with any question about faith is, "I know what the Bible says. I believe it. That settles it."

Which faith style does Jamal represent?

In my reading of Jamal, I placed him as being still in the experienced faith style. Why?

I'm wary of his easy answers and take note that he is still a concrete thinker. Jamal is not yet demonstrating his ability to think critically. He's not searching, and he is seeking to affiliate. What is your best response to Jamal?

Continue to engage him with questions that begin to move him from concrete to abstract thinking. ("What if" questions do this best.) Listen and be patient.

What is your worst response to Jamal? Telling Jamal that he's being "narrow-minded" or demanding and that he should be less judgmental will only reinforce his rigidity and threaten him. He won't open up. He'll clamp down even harder.

2. Michele used to be active and strong in the church, and now, in her senior year in high school, she is battling having to come to anything. She is questioning everything about the church and the faith of her parents. This is driving her parents crazy. Church is important to them, and they want their whole family to come to worship. Michele, when she does show up, prefers to sit in the car in the parking lot and listen to music.

Which faith style does Michele represent?

If you thought "searching," you're right on it. It sounds like she's in a doubt/critical judgment form in the searching faith style. Why?

The key is that Michele used to be active and strong. She's growing up and questioning her church and its beliefs and separating from her family. What is your best response to Michele?

Have a conversation with her and let her know that questioning is okay and a vital part of the journey. Check in with her from time to time. You'll need to do some major care for her parents, too. They're the ones who are struggling the most with this. Plead with them to keep communication lines open.

What is your worst response to Michele? To demand that she participate or to tell her that questioning is wrong will cut communication lines, and then, as she makes her way through this faith style, she'll have nowhere to turn.

3. Denise loves to sing the praise songs she learned years ago. When friends tell her they're having problems, she tells them to "let go and let God." She reads her Bible often, listens to Christian music, and quotes Scripture verses frequently.

Which faith style does Denise represent?

There are options here. Without more information, the case could be made that Denise is in an owned faith style. The case could also be made that Denise is still in an experienced faith style. Why?

She could be in an owned faith style because she seems to have a good sense of her own faith. But her use of the cliché "Let go and let God" may indicate that she is actually in an experienced faith style where she is simply parroting back words and phrases she has heard from others. Many young people and adults are stunted in their growth and remain in the experienced faith style. Denise may be one of them. What is your best response to Denise?

Engage Denise in conversation. Does she really believe the cliché? What does it mean to her in her own words? Is there evidence that she has thought about its meaning and has appropriated it for her own life? Someone in an owned faith style would be able to articulate what the phrase means with depth and authenticity. If she cannot, then she will need your help in moving beyond an experienced faith style.

What is your worst response to Denise? To simply take everything she says at face value ignores the very real possibility that her growth is stunted.

4. Carlos came to youth group saying he was sick and tired of all the talking and wants the group to do something. He has a friend whose youth group is sponsoring a child through a Christian organization. He thinks the youth group should decide to do the same thing tonight. When you suggest the group gather some information and talk about it next week, he says, "See? That's what I'm saying. All we do is talk about stuff! We never do anything!"

Which faith style does Carlos represent?

Clearly Carlos is seeking to affiliate and to commit to persons and/or causes. Why?

Carlos wants to do something and to make a difference. He's impatient. He's eager to see what being a Christian looks like. What is your best response to Carlos?

Your trying to gather more information was a nice gesture, but it didn't work with him. If the group is willing, it's perfectly acceptable for Carlos to bring up the possibility of sponsoring a child now. Wait and see where the Holy Spirit leads. Any offering of passion and energy around a cause needs to be taken seriously and accepted quickly—even when that offering comes from the same person about a different cause week to week.

What is your worst response to Carlos? If you dismiss him or put off a decision, Carlos will see that not as a stalling tactic but as inactivity and a lack of commitment. He won't stay long.

5. Keisha, a high school junior, grew up in the church and was recently ordained an elder. She shares her faith freely and honestly. Last weekend, one of her best friends died in a car accident. She is devastated and comes to you asking, "Where was God in my friend's death?"

What faith style does Keisha represent?

Keisha was in an owned faith style and is now entering a searching faith style. Why?

Her election as elder is a clue that Keisha was in an owned faith situation—with a faith that truly belonged to her. The question in the midst of her grief around her friend's death shows that she is back in a searching style, which is an honest place to be. What is your best response to Keisha?

Respond with open, honest, and heartfelt conversation. Assure her that God was with her best friend in her dying and that her best friend is with God. Tell her that God's heart was the first heart to break in the death of her friend. Be pastoral and present.

What is your worst response to Keisha? Sometimes when our "solid kids" show any sign of weakness, we are either shocked or come down harder on them than on others. That's not fair. Keisha deserves and needs as much grace as anyone—as we ourselves do. Statements like "But Keisha, your faith was so strong. Why are you doubting?" do nothing but hurt and isolate.

6. Carter, who only last year was a quiet little boy, is starting to grow and mature rapidly. He always comes to church school early because his parents teach other classes. Last week he walked in and, for the first time, took the initiative by asking if there was anything he could do to help. You gave him several tasks. Today he walked in and said he enjoyed helping out last week and wants to do more.

What faith style does Carter represent?

Carter is seeking to belong in the affiliative faith style. Why? It's clear that Carter is searching out his own identity (*the* primary developmental task for adolescents) by finding an appropriate role in relationship to you. He tried an identity of just getting to church early and doing nothing, and it didn't fit. Now he's trying a new identity of helping you, and it seems to fit better. What is your best response to Carter?

Continue to find meaningful opportunities for Carter to belong and thank him for his kindness. Be encouraging and remind Carter from time to time that he truly belongs.

What is your worst response to Carter? To tell him that his help is not needed or to take him for granted will not increase his sense of belonging.

7. Amanda's stepmother phoned frantic because Amanda was in her room burning incense and meditating. She's listening to some New Age tape about getting "in touch with your inner soul." She also is reading a *Book of Mormon* one of her friends loaned to her. Once her stepmom overheard Amanda talk about the satanic bible during a phone conversation.

Which faith style does Amanda represent?

Amanda is in the searching faith style in the experimentation form in a big way. Why?

This faith style is evident in her meditating, reading the *Book of Mormon*, and delving into New Age mysticism. These are all healthy signs of experimentation. Amanda is simply seeing what else is out there and trying it on. What is your best response to Amanda?

Be patient. First, you'll need to calm down Amanda's stepmother. Why not take this as a cue to lead some sessions on other faith systems in church school or youth group? Show Amanda that you're open to conversations. Check in with her gently but intentionally. Don't let her wander around out there on her own. Be present with her as much as possible—if not physically then certainly spiritually—and let her know that you're with her.

What is your worst response to Amanda? Any attempt to prevent her from experimenting will be a disaster. There is no "magic" in the *Book of Mormon* that will make Amanda become a Mormon any more than reading the Bible will make a person a Christian. Still, experimentation can become dangerous if it threatens her health and well-being. That's why communication lines have to be open so you can know what is happening with her.

8. Dexter gets bored whenever you open the Bible. His body language is obvious. He crosses his arms, drops his head, and slumps over. But given the chance, Dexter loves to write original songs, sing, draw pictures, create videos, paint, play the guitar, dance, you name it—all about his faith in Christ and love of God and trust in the Holy Spirit. But when it comes to Bible study, he's not there. When you ask him why he shuts down whenever you open the Bible, he responds, "I don't know. It's just that it all seems so boring."

Which faith style does Dexter represent?

Dexter is in the affiliative faith style, subheading "Affections." Why?

It's clear that for Dexter, he is in a place where his heart is moved by faith and his head is not. This is a tough place to be because much of what we do around faith focuses on the head rather than the heart. All the things he enjoys doing relate more to the heart than the head. What is your best response to Dexter?

Bible study is important, but are there ways you can incorporate song and dance and art and other expressions in your study of Scripture? Of course there are! Blend head and heart so that Dexter can see the value in both. Further, find ways for Dexter to offer his gifts to the whole congregation.

What is your worst response to Dexter? Trying to force him to participate or scolding him for not paying attention won't help. That's not where he is. Also, giving any sense that thinking is more important than feeling will be a dismissal of where Dexter is in his faith.

It's important to say that in all these scenarios, your best response starts and ends with prayer. When we pray, we remind ourselves that it truly is not our will but God's will at work in us. Our young people don't even need to know that we're praying for them. If you're fortunate enough to be part of a team of leaders (both adults and youth), then divide up your young people so that everyone is being prayed for on a regular basis.

As you can see, knowing these faith styles helps give another perspective on how young people live out their faith in our midst. Consider sharing these faith styles with parents, stepparents, and other teachers and leaders so that they, too, may become familiar with them. This chapter has explored much of the inner workings of faith development with young people, thanks to the fine work of John Westerhoff. But we know that young people are greatly affected by what is happening outside of them as well. The next chapter explores how the outside "youth culture" impacts our ministry with young people.

2
The Youth Culture

"Have young people changed all that much in the past forty years?" "Are young people all that different from their parents?" "All I know is that what used to work with young people doesn't work today. Why is that?" Throughout my travels around the church, these are the kinds of questions I'm asked. And I've come to the conclusion that what used to work in youth ministry in many places no longer works, not so much because young people as a generation are different but rather because the world in which young people are growing up today is so markedly different. It's true. Even when I talk with youth ministry leaders who are only ten or fifteen years out of high school, they tell me that the high school young people in their congregation are facing a different world than the world they knew in high school. This different world is called the "youth culture." While sociologists debate whether this is truly a distinct subculture, those who minister to and care about young people need to be aware of the major trends facing the youth of today.

Trends versus Fads

Remember that we are not simply talking about *fads*. Fads are vastly different from *trends*. Fads are short-lived, often manufactured by a designer or marketer or entertainer, and they contradict previous fads. While they may appear to affect the whole population, ultimately they affect a smaller group. In contrast, a trend is long-term. Trends build on previous trends rather than contradicting them. Trends emerge from the grass roots rather than being invented and affect a huge percentage of the population. Given these differences between trends and fads, I propose the following six trends and discuss their implications for the church's ministry with young people.

Six Trends in the Youth Culture
1. Young people have more choices than ever before.

One reason the old model of youth ministry no longer works is that young people have more choices than ever before. Years ago, when the church held a meeting for young people, most went because there was little else to do. Today, young people have a variety of ways to spend their time. The church is in direct competition with school events, athletic events, work, family demands, and any number of entertainment opportunities. More young people have access to cars than ever before, making them far more mobile as a generation. Young people can choose to attend different schools than their parents and stepparents. Young people can choose different occupations. Not all these choices are bad. It's wonderful, for instance, that young women can choose to be physicians, as well as nurses, and pilots, as well as flight attendants, but the increase in choices has been dramatic and will likely continue. Consider television as an example of the dramatic increase in choices. Years ago, there were three network channels available with a fourth public station in larger communities. Today, through cable and satellite hookups, people can choose from hundreds of channels that broadcast twenty-four hours a day. In the near future, with the World Wide Web coming to television, those choices will further increase.

2. Young people are growing up in a more violent society.

The last poll of adolescents I read said that 44 percent of young people in the United States have ready access to a handgun and 33 percent go to school fearful for their personal safety. Those percentages continue to rise. That over four in ten young people feel they can readily obtain a handgun and that one-third of students across the country are afraid in school are alarming statistics. The Centers for Disease Control report that homicide is now the third leading killer of adolescents in the United States.

These statistics and others point to the fact that young people are living in a more violent society. Incidences of reported child abuse and spouse abuse are also on the rise. Clearly, this is a generation accustomed to violence and for whom violence is a daily expectation. This *is* a different world from the world in which parents and stepparents grew up. While there have always been fights in school, today's fights are more likely to end in gun shots. While there have always been gangs and secret clubs in neighborhoods and schools, today's gangs take on a new level of importance because money and drugs may be involved and retribution or retaliation in the form of drive-by shootings and killings is not unusual. Even our congregations are not immune to this violence because the young people in our churches are very much a part of the world in which this violence happens.

3. The media impact continues to grow.

Remarkably, television-watching time appears to be dropping among high schoolers. This is largely because they have so little free time. Even so, the impact of the media on young people's lives is dramatic. Television watching for children and early adolescents does consume a great deal of time. All ages spend more time watching videos than ever before. And what time is not spent with the television is likely spent listening to the radio, CDs, or DAT, or sitting at the computer surfing the Internet. As a result of this huge media impact, young people today are more visually oriented than ever. They are used to seeing bright, colorful images that engage quickly and change just as rapidly. This obviously affects attention span. Educators and researchers continue to document a declining attention span among young people.

Even more remarkable, there is an emerging body of research that indicates more young people are able to "multitask" or give "parallel attention" to a variety of tasks simultaneously. Whereas previous generations sought to eliminate all other stimuli so they could concentrate on one thing at a time, this generation may actually need to have several things happening at once to keep their attention going on anything. Such a dramatic shift has huge implications on how we engage young people in worship, church school, youth group, and so forth.

4. The family pattern is changing.

The Children's Defense Fund reports that one-third of all children born today will spend part of their childhood in a single-parent home. They also project that by the year 2004 the number of nontraditional households with children (those with single parents, stepparents, or gay couples) will outnumber traditional households with children (both biological parents in the home). Further, the number of traditional households with both parents working full-time is on the rise. So even if a young person has both parents at home, they are both likely to be busy at work.

The bottom line? Children and young people today endure more hours unsupervised by an adult during a given day than any generation in our history. The family configuration is changing dramatically. All families seem to indicate that "family time" is a precious commodity. The latest Gallup poll says that teenagers eat an average of three meals per week with the family. Many young people with whom I've talked are surprised that it is that high!

5. Young people are growing up in a fast-food society.

The nature of the world today is one of instant gratification. Nothing nurtures this expectation more than the fast-food industry. The promise of the industry is food that is fast, cheap, and convenient. Growing up in this kind of world, young people more and more are expecting this same kind of experience from much of their life. Education is treated as more of a "fast-food" experience. Information is given in "sound bites." Deeper, more profound understandings are discouraged. Students read and study to get something out of it as quickly as possible, then move on to the next task. This instant gratification mentality carries over into the church. That you "ought to get something out of it" becomes the basic requirement. If the church doesn't do anything for you, why show up?

Further, the fast-food society leads to a disposable society. Today, we use and then dispose of everything from plates, forks, and spoons to cameras, diapers, and contact lenses. It is not that far a leap for young people to begin to see relationships and commitments as disposable as well. In a fast-food society, where the ultimate measure of worth is whether or not *you* get anything out of it, then values such as commitment and constancy matter little.

6. Young people are developing a narrow worldview.

It is a great irony that while dramatic advances in communications and transportation technology appear to have made the whole world smaller in the sense that it is much more accessible to every person in the United States, more of our young people are developing a narrow worldview in that they seem to view only their immediate world with any value and concern. One leader told me it's like the young people have "blinders on to anything outside of their neighborhood. They just don't seem to care what's happening in the rest of the world." This is often manifested in a "let's take care of our own first" kind of thinking.

I encountered this thinking years ago while working with a group of adults and young people to decide who would be the recipients of our conference offering. The strongest voices for giving the money to a local charity came from the young people. It was only a few adults who expressed the hope that the money might be sent to a partner church in another country for their use. The concern expressed by the young people was simply that "we have needy people here. Let other people take care of their own." When I mentioned that we are the wealthiest nation in the world and that Christ's call to his disciples was to care for the stranger, the response from some of the young people was that other Americans were no less strangers than those in other countries and "deserved" no less. Eventually, we compromised and divided the offering evenly between a domestic recipient and an international one.

Implications

Given these cultural trends, it's important that we examine their implications for our work in youth ministry.

1. Young people have more choices than ever before.

Given the trend that young people have more choices than ever before and building on the assumption that these choices will likely continue to grow, leaders in youth ministry need to do the following:

- Offer young people opportunities to make good choices. With a world filled with options, we need to offer choices in our ministry with young people so they may hone their decision-making skills. Leading young people through a planning process helps them make choices. Enabling young people to lead portions of sessions helps them develop their decision-making skills. For every choice that is made, young people must be helped to see consequences for decisions.

- Use decision-making language more consistently. I was greatly impressed by one of our associate pastors in Texas who makes it a point to comment on the choices her young people are making. Phrases like "Good choice, Angel," "Interesting choice, Natalie," and "Hmm, why did you make that choice, Denise?" flow freely throughout any gathering of young people. Consequently, others in the group have picked up the same language. These young people realize they have moment-by-moment choices, and they're making decisions out of good practice and good affirmation. Further, these young people are growing in the sense of their own power. Most young people feel as if they have no personal power. By naming the choices they do have and the consequences of those choices, we're helping young people realize that they do have power in their own lives and that what they choose makes a difference.

2. Young people are growing up in a more violent society.

Given the trend that young people are growing up in a more violent society and building on the assumption that the violence will continue, leaders in youth ministry can help in these ways:

- Ensure that the community of faith is a safe, secure place. Safety and security are crucial issues for human beings. If a person does not feel safe and secure, fear will be an all-consuming factor that hinders participation in a group. The first task of youth ministry leaders, both youth and adults, is to ensure that the group is a safe place. This means that persons know they will not be ridiculed or hurt or abused. Establishing a group covenant will be important so that all participants know what is expected of them (see chapter 5). Further, leaders must act quickly to stop any behavior that prevents a person from feeling safe and secure in the group. On a regular basis, state openly that you hope this is a "safe and secure place for everyone." Listen for their responses, both verbal and nonverbal. They will tell you if they feel it is a safe and secure place.

- Help young people envision realistic alternatives to violence. One of the great challenges in working with young people is overcoming the common sentiment that "that's just the way it is" and nothing can be done to change it. For a generation that has grown up with violence on their television screens and for many in their neighborhoods, this is a common way of thinking. Still, leaders must help young people envision an alternative to a world filled with violence. The Presbyterian Peacemaking Program has an outstanding six-session minicourse titled *Youth and Peacemaking*. This minicourse is designed to help young people cope with the violence in their world. The program sessions also help young people identify alternatives to violence in their own lives and in society. Several stories are included of young people who have made a tremendous impact on their own towns and cities. I commend it to you and have included order information in the bibliography.

3. The media impact continues to grow.

Given the trend that the media impact continues to grow with young people, leaders in youth ministry can do the following to help counteract media influence:

- Help young people develop critical viewing skills. I received a phone call one Monday morning from a parent who was asking questions from the "national office" on whether it was appropriate for a youth director to show an "R"-rated video to a group of middle-schoolers. I could tell right away this woman was fishing for

Sowing the Seeds

"ammunition" and that the youth director, whom I did not know, was in trouble. We talked through the incident, and I told her about the need to help young people view the media critically. Thankfully, the youth director did debrief the video after viewing it. They spent significant time talking about the movie and its themes and even related it to a biblical passage. By the end of the conversation, I think I had helped her understand what it means to help young people learn critical viewing skills. Honestly, aside from pornography and films filled with gratuitous sex and violence, I can justify seeing almost any film if we talk about it before and after from a critical viewpoint. This approach models for young people how we cannot just take everything in. We must be thinking about what we see and hear through a screen given to us through our faith in Jesus Christ.

• Develop their own media to speak for their own generation. I was at a conference where a presenter was pushing us about how we work with the media impact on young people. When he asked what we should be doing, I shared the need to develop critical viewing skills. He agreed but wanted us to go further. "Why teach them just to be good consumers of the culture?" he asked. "Why not teach them to be creators of their own culture as well?" Why not indeed! His comment sparked in me the need to help our young people not just to learn how to view critically what the culture gives them, but to create, to find their own voices.

With video cameras and sophisticated recording devices and inexpensive mixers available, many young people are forming bands and writing songs and poetry and screenplays. Encourage this. Encourage them to create their own media to say what they want to say and show what they want to show. Then gather groups to see and hear what they have created. One presbytery has an evening when any band can sign up to come play. They limit each band to two or three songs. The bands all come from congregations in the presbytery, and the youth groups come in huge numbers both to support their own and to hear what others are creating. It's a wonderful evening! In this way, young people are being helped to be creators of culture rather than simply consumers of culture.

4. The family pattern is changing.

Given the trend that the family pattern is changing, leaders need to include the following in their youth ministry:

- Ensure that their language reflects the variety of family patterns in the group. Watch your language! With fewer and fewer young people growing up in the traditional family (with both biological parents in the home), we can no longer be talking only about "parents." Include stepparents and caregivers in your language when you describe families. This is more than just trying to be "politically correct." Language shapes our world, and when a young person who lives with his or her mother and stepfather never hears the term, he or she begins to believe that he or she is somehow less than acceptable, and this increases feelings of inadequacy, embarrassment, and shame. If at all possible, make home visits. Being in a home communicates a vast amount of information about the young person's daily life. Further, talking with parents and stepparents opens a link of communication that will be helpful in the future.

- Include the whole family in ministry. One of the best and most remarkable trends in youth ministry is the reconfiguring of job descriptions and responsibilities to include the families of young people. We know that no child is an island. Families have an extraordinary impact on their children's lives. When a young person is struggling, in most cases the family is struggling, too. Spend time in the group addressing family struggles and conflicts. Affirm families and build in specific times to meet with parents and stepparents. Often these caregivers are desperate for support and help in coping with their adolescents. Include a program time each quarter when parents and children come together to learn communication, relationship-building, and conflict-resolution skills.

5. Young people are growing up in a fast-food society.

Given we are in a society of instant gratification, leaders in youth ministry need to provide opportunities for young people to see a project through from beginning to end. The classic fast-food view is summarized in the conversation between a granddaughter who disagreed with her grandfather when he was explaining how you milk cows. "Grandpa," she said incredulously, "you're fibbing. Everyone knows milk comes from the store!" That's the view of many young people today. Living in a disposable society means it happens here and now, and there is no before and no after. Helping young people see a project through from beginning to end helps them see the whole picture, not just a snapshot. Mission trips and other mission activities, assembling gift baskets, and so forth, illustrate this concept beautifully. Why not put up a timeline around your meeting area and mark off each step of the way?

Helping young people see the big picture will also help them build their patience level and keep them on the task. They'll be amazed at what they've accomplished over the long term. Be especially careful that you are not feeding the fast-food mentality with your programs. I was talking with an associate pastor from one of our large churches in Charlotte, North Carolina. He had his young people scheduled a mile a minute because they demanded that to keep interested. "When do you stop and breathe and reflect?" I asked him. "When do you go off on a hillside and pray?"

"There's no time," he said. "My kids are the busiest kids, and I've got to compete with school and other influences."

"You know," I told him, "I understand your wanting to keep them engaged in the life of the church, but I can't help worrying that you're contributing to the pattern of the fast-food world in which they live. My hope would be that we offer them an alternative."

His last words to me were "Are you kidding? Add something else? We don't have time!"

We are called to offer an alternative. Certainly we offer fun activities to keep young people attracted, but the program must be balanced so that we are not driving youth and ourselves into a tragic pattern of burnout.

6. Young people are developing a narrow worldview.

Given the trend that as technology has made our world smaller so have our views of and interest in global affairs narrowed, leaders in youth ministry need to connect young people to something bigger than their narrow worldview. While I was in Wyoming speaking at a presbytery event, I had coffee with a group of pastors and lay leaders of youth ministry. We were talking about the Presbyterian Youth Triennium, a gathering of more than six thousand youth and adults. I was remarking about how this tiny presbytery with just twenty-two churches scattered throughout the entire state manages to send almost as many delegates as some of our huge urban presbyteries with six times as many churches. "It's simple," said one of the leaders. "We need it more."

"What do you mean?" I asked.

"Look at us. Some of us drive six hours to get to a presbytery meeting. We're so spread out, we have no idea that we're part of something bigger. My kids come to Triennium just to walk into the auditorium. For some of us, there are more people there than live in our town."

She was right. The gift of events like the Triennium is that young people gain a sense of the wider church. It happens at presbytery events, synod events, General Assembly events, and world events. It's that feeling of being connected to something bigger than just you— that feeling that you are not alone in this. What a remarkable gift to know you are not alone. So, do whatever you can to break your group out of its own little world. Go anywhere, whenever, to get them to connect with others so they realize they are not alone.

Too often not just young people, but the whole of a congregation's youth ministry, are isolated. Too often there is this sense that youth ministry is off somewhere else. Just as we are called to be connected to something bigger than ourselves, we are called to be connected to the whole congregation as well. The next chapter explores how we integrate the young people into the life of the church.

3

Integrating Young
People into the
Whole Life of the Church

I was leading a workshop in Chicago on incorporating young people into the full life of the church. When I raised the point about inviting young people to be liturgists on a regular basis, rather than only ushers, one of the pastors raised his hand and asked, "But isn't that what Youth Sunday is for?" His question illustrates my discomfort with designating one Sunday in a year as Youth Sunday. Too many churches approach Youth Sunday as the obligatory task for the young people in the church to take over the worship service, do something fun and cute (and hopefully theologically sound) so the church can say they value young people and want them to be full members in the life of the congregation. That's not the purpose of Youth Sunday.

From the denomination's viewpoint, Youth Sunday, or officially, Young People in the Church Sunday, is a special designation to encourage the congregation to pause and celebrate the particular gifts of young people in the life of the church. Looking at the Presbyterian Program Planning Calendar, or any denominational planning calendar for that matter, you'll see a series of different designations for each Sunday. The purpose of these various emphases is to bring a particular ministry or need to the congregation's attention. That's the hope of any Sunday recognizing young people. Its purpose is not to form some kind of a checklist so the congregation can say, "There, we've done that emphasis. Whew! Glad that's over with for the year!" In fact, while I support the opportunity to focus on particular ministries throughout the year, I know of several congregations who have young people so involved in the congregation's worship (including preaching quarterly) that they've done away with the Youth Sunday. Those congregations are doing an extraordinary job of incorporating young people into the full life of the church. That's really what youth ministry is about.

Youth ministry is not just the youth group meeting. It's not just the church school class. Youth ministry happens wherever and whenever young people are involved in the life of the church. One of the worst things we do as youth ministry leaders is to perpetuate this idea that youth ministry is specific to a program. It is not. Too often I've heard church leaders say, "We have a terrific youth ministry. Our youth group is growing by leaps and bounds and meets weekly." When I ask what else is happening in their ministry with youth, they're perplexed. For them, youth group meetings are the totality of their ministry with young people. My response? You've missed it. That's not what youth ministry is about. You're no doubt running a wonderful, faithful youth program. But a youth program or a youth group is only one component of a dynamic ministry with youth.

Integrating Youth Ministry into the Church's Building

Whenever I visit a church building, I love to walk around and see the sanctuary, different classrooms, offices, and so on. If I have a chance, I enjoy having young people as tour guides. They tell marvelous stories. I was visiting a church in Seattle and when we passed a room, my young tour guide said, "Oh, and that's the parlor. We can't go in there. They're afraid we'll break stuff."

"What?" I asked incredulously.

"I said," she repeated, "we're not allowed in there. This is really too bad because they have great couches and it'd be a lot better sleeping on those couches than on the floor during lock-ins."

I told her, "C'mon," and together we walked into the room and looked around. It was a beautiful room with lovely furniture and paintings and lamps and draperies. I could see that it was very tastefully decorated, but it burned me up that young people were excluded from the space. The message being sent was clear. We value these things more than we value you.

My tour continued on to the youth room. The youth room was in the basement of the church in the farthest corner away from the stairwell. It had tiny frosted windows at the top of the walls. The room was painted with bright colors, and posters were on most of the walls. The couches, though, were clearly donated and in bad condition. The carpet was an old shag and was dirty. There was a broken Ping-Pong table in a corner. Someone had donated an old stereo system. They had done a great job making a terrible space liveable and useable. "It's sorta dingy," I remember my tour guide saying, "but we like it because it's our space."

She was right. It was their space and that's important. Young people need to know they have a place they belong in the church, but why does that space have to be the darkest, dingiest, and farthest space in the church? And why are there spaces they are not allowed to visit even though many of them are full members of the church?

Integration is more than enabling young people to lead in worship on a regular basis. Integration is making any meeting space for youth accessible and visible for the congregation, with furnishings that equal the finest room in the building. Young people are tough on furniture, no question. But today there are stain-resistant carpets and stain-resistant furniture that are as attractive as they are tough and durable.

Engaging Youth in Church Governance

Beyond integrating young people's space into the life of the whole church, young people need to be included in the governance of the church. After becoming a member of the congregation, young people are fully eligible to be officers of the church. In fact, for the Presbyterian Church, the denomination has made a special exception to encourage congregations to elect young people even when they may not be able to serve a full term of three years. (See the *Book of Order,* G-14.0201a.) Any governing body of a congregation, be it a session, board, or consistory, should reflect the ages of those whom it governs. This means calling young people to serve according to the leading of the Holy Spirit. Slowly, this is a growing practice among many churches.

In 1992 at the Presbyterian Youth Triennium, we needed two hundred and fifty elders to serve communion for the closing worship service. We issued the call with a preference for young people who were ordained as elders, but we invited adults also, certain we would not have enough young people among the gathering of nearly six thousand. I was surprised when we got to the rehearsal. We ended up sending all the adults away because they weren't needed. We had just over two hundred and fifty young people present. So when the celebrant invited the "elders of the church to come forward" to serve the people, two hundred and fifty-seven youth stood up and approached the platform. Later, one of the adults sitting in the congregation told me she heard young people around her exclaim, "Hey, look! They're all kids. Cool!"

It is an important witness to young people and to the whole church when a young person is called as a leader. It's part of the sign of integrating young people into the whole life of the church. If offering a place on a church session or board doesn't seem possible, seek to have young people serve on various committees and task forces—certainly on the congregation's nominating committee and especially on any nominating committee seeking a youth ministry director or associate pastor with specific responsibilities for youth ministry.

One of my good friends was seeking a call as an associate pastor. He has wonderful skills in youth ministry, and he wanted that to be his main focus. He was pursued by several churches. After looking over all of them, he quickly dismissed those whose search committees did not include young people. "It told me that they didn't take the empowerment of young people seriously," he said. In fact, he ended up being called to a congregation who had co-chairs of their pastor nominating committee. A businessman from the church was one of the chairpersons. The other? A sixteen-year-old high school junior.

Connecting Young People to the Whole Church

Two years ago the Presbyterian Church (U.S.A.) launched its new youth ministry organization called the Presbyterian Youth Connection. The Presbyterian Youth Connection has five intentions as its theological and philosophical foundation. The fourth intention listed is "to be connected to the whole church, community, world." I'm impressed with this intention. It says that young people are to be connected to the *whole* church—not just to a youth group or a church school class.

So, involve young people everywhere: worship, mission, governance, education, fellowship, you name it. And at every opportunity, interpret where young people are involved in the church's life. Why does there have to be a separate newsletter just for young people? Include copies nested in the congregation's newsletter or better yet, include their information on a page so that *everyone* knows what is happening with young people. Integration of the youth ministry into the whole life of the church is not a simple task. It is a whole different mindset from what many of us have been doing. I am convinced it is crucial for the future of the church.

4

What to Do with the Church School?

In her wonderful book *Surveying the Land*, my good friend Lynn Turnage writes that "church school is a place to learn about Jesus Christ, a systematic way of exploring issues related to the faith, an easy, comfortable, and safe place to learn, a place to explore and express faith-related issues." For many years, church school was the single opportunity for our children and youth to grow in their faith in Christ. Now, for many congregations, church school is in serious crisis.

For years we have operated with the erroneous assumption that church school is only for children and youth. This has led to a serious lack of church school opportunities for adults. To be sure, there are many congregations who are growing dynamic educational opportunities for adults, but most of us have been slow to pick up the challenge of offering as many classes for adults as we do for children and youth. This has led to a "drop-off" pattern, wherein parents and stepparents drop off their children and youth for church school and only come for worship. In some cases, these adults don't even attend worship. Ultimately, this model doesn't last long, as young people, in their natural questioning and challenging role (remember Westerhoff's searching faith style?), begin to ask why it's so important that they have to attend church school but their parents and stepparents do not. After a while, parents tell me, the battle is just not worth it, and the young people quit going.

Role of the Church School

Worship is at the heart of our tradition. But also at the heart of our tradition is a call from God to engage our minds in the study of God's word. We live in a day and a time when the complex issues of life call us to deeper understanding and intentional study of the Word. Issues and questions that our ancient writers and theologians could not have even imagined are at the center of debates today. We cannot access these deeper understandings and intentional study by ourselves. We continue to need the community of faith to both hold us accountable and encourage us. That's the role that the church school class plays. Church school is different from youth group, where the major focus is on fellowship and group building. The purpose of the church school is to provide a setting for intentional learning. For any ministry with youth, there must be an opportunity for young people to engage in serious study and reflection of Scripture. With so many church schools facing dwindling numbers of adolescents, we need a new model for this intentional study.

Intentional Study When and Where Young People Are Available

One of the key understandings today must be that ministry can happen only when and where people are available. At one time in our nation's history, 9:30 A.M. on Sunday was when young people were available and the church building was where young people were. For many communities today, however, that is no longer true. We're still operating as if the old days were with us. We're still relying on an old model for intentional study.

Certainly attendance is no measure of faithfulness by itself, but we are seeking to provide an opportunity for study for as many of our young people as possible. Look at your church school class. What percent of your young people participate on a regular basis? If your percentage is more than 60 percent, you're actually doing quite well. Keep the class going and be thankful! If you're below 60 percent (most of us are well below this number), it's time for a new model. It's time to consider another place and another time for your intentional study.

Gather a core group of young people, most likely the faithful few who have been gathering for church school, and talk about the possibilities. From this core group, gain a commitment to try something new and to contact other members of the congregation who haven't been coming but might be interested.

A number of years ago I was in Portland, Oregon, for a presbytery retreat, and one associate pastor asked if I'd like to come to their church school class. He said it started at 7:30 A.M., on Saturday. I thought he was joking. He picked me up at 7:00 A.M. and we made our way to the church. When we walked in, the smell of bacon and pancakes hit us. Sipping a cup of coffee, I watched as a crew of four retired men cooked up a mound of hot food for breakfast. These men came from the men's group of the church and did this every Saturday morning. It was fun listening to their bantering back and forth.

At 7:20, there was no one else in the building except the four cooks, me, and the associate pastor. I looked at him a little skeptically.

At 7:25, the first group of young people arrived with Bibles in hand. At 7:30, there were thirty-five of them sitting around tables, drinking coffee, Coke, and Mountain Dew. The men were moving around the tables serving mounds of hot pancakes, eggs, bacon, and fruit. By now they knew many of the young people and were known by them. I was amazed.

After twenty minutes of eating, the associate opened with a fifteen-minute talk about the passage they were studying in Ephesians. There were a few questions and comments. Then they went into study groups for thirty minutes. By 8:45, they were gone, and we were helping to clean up. Later the associate pastor told me it was all their idea. "They want to sleep in on Sunday because most of them are out late on Saturday night," he told me. "Their Saturdays are filled with activities and they have to be up and out by 10:00 A.M. anyway, so they suggested this."

Many other congregations have switched the church school class to a Wednesday night when the rest of the congregation is engaged in study as well. The evening begins with a light meal and is over by 8:00 P.M. sharp so young people can head home to do homework. Only you can know when and where young people are most available. Homes seem very attractive to this generation as a meeting place. Consider gathering in a home or several homes if you're organized into smaller Bible study groups. Remember the test questions: When are young people most available and where? Find out and meet at that time in the place they suggest.

It's important as we reexamine the time and place of intentional study that we also reconsider the style of intentional study. We are moving away from a style that focused on the teacher in a lecture format to a style where every person is engaged in the study and the learning. This active participation is what young people seem to respond to and value the most. As you issue the call to adult leaders, be sure you consider their style of leadership. As you choose a curriculum for their use, be sure you consider the style of learning used in the curriculum.

Curriculum Checklist

Consider the following eight basic characteristics as the start to a checklist for any curriculum you choose for your intentional study time.

1. *User-friendly*—Most teachers have little extra time to prepare. A session plan that calls on teachers to spend any more than an hour in preparation is unreasonable. Likewise beware of a curriculum that advertises no preparation time.

2. Visual—This is a visual generation, and visual young people need visual teaching. Your curriculum should constantly be offering something for the learner to see.

3. Self-contained—Any curriculum that expects young people to be present from week to week or to do outside reading or remember a lesson from three weeks ago was written at a time when we could rely on the same young people gathering and faithfully doing homework for church school. In a few communities this still exists, but for the vast majority, a curriculum must be self-contained, meaning it does not depend on the student being present last week for him or her to understand what is happening this week.

4. Multicultural—The world in which young people are growing up is multicultural even though most of our churches are not. Still, the curriculum should reflect a view of the world in which many cultures are not dominated by any one culture. The curriculum should give equal weight to Native Americans, African Americans, Hispanic people, Asian Americans, and Anglo-Americans.

5. Activity-oriented—Most young people, especially early adolescents, need something to do. That's why many find intentional study to be so boring. There is emerging evidence that this is a multitask generation, which means they can do several things at once and be paying attention at the same time. Your curriculum should involve the learner actively.

6. Discussion-based—Young people are full of opinions, and most are willing and eager to share them in a safe environment. They're eager to engage in meaningful conversations, to be heard. Choose a curriculum that provides for meaningful discussions. Older adolescents especially will find this valuable.

7. Bible-oriented—It's a personal bias of mine that any curriculum should direct young people to the Bible so they can hone their skills in working with the text. If your curriculum prints the biblical text for them, it deprives them of an opportunity to read it from the Bible itself. Each time young people open the Bible, they become more familiar with it. Avoid curricula that print the text.

8. Youth-led—Young people must be taken seriously as leaders. After all, they're not required to be present for this time. Choose a curriculum that does not simply assume that adults are always in charge of everything. If your curriculum provides opportunities for young people to serve as leadership or, better yet, assumes that youth are leading the study, it will be better received.

Important Practices

Here are few hints for leaders as you approach your intentional study time.

1. Get there early and have something for the early arrivals to do. The most awkward time for those who don't know anyone else in the group is when they have just arrived and there is nothing to do. As the leader, be there early so no one will just sit there. Greet each person and invite him or her to a snack or to a task or to talk with someone else.

2. Remember that the environment teaches. Give some attention to your meeting space. Change a poster or post a question. Do anything visual to add to the space and give a hint of the study for the session.

3. Use every opportunity to open the Bible. If you're unsure of your Bible recall skills, have a good concordance on hand.

4. Push the application question: So what does this have to do with me?

5. Open and close with prayer. Remember, there is great power in modeling a meaningful routine. If it won't cause too much disruption, invite group members to join hands.

One more suggestion . . .

Whenever you gather, check in. After you have opened with prayer, be sure everyone in the group has been introduced by name. Ask each person to think of one highlight from this past week and one lowlight. Share one or the other first, or invite each person to share both. Either ask for a volunteer or start yourself. Move around the circle encouraging each person to share. Share these highlights and lowlights every time you gather so that even those who may attend class only twice a year will know this part of the routine. This may sound like fellowship and group building, and it is. But remember that young people for the most part are social creatures. They won't be able to listen until they've checked in with each other and met the newcomers. Move this check-in time along so it doesn't consume the meeting time. It will prove important to the group's life and will help open the group for deeper discussions.

Routines such as this one help provide stability for young people— something many are lacking in their lives. Sometimes lack of stability results in acting out in the group. Over the years, I've begun receiving more and more requests for what to do with young people whose behavior is a problem. The next chapter focuses on that specific issue.

5
Managing Problem Behaviors

The call came from an associate pastor in Milwaukee. He started off apologizing right away. "I'm really sorry to bother you about this, but I really need your help," he said. He then moved into a description of a troubled fifteen-year-old in his church school class and youth group. The previous Sunday, when he was asked for the fifth time to be quiet and listen, the young man got up, said a few choice words to the teacher, threw his chair against the wall, and stomped out of class. I assured the pastor that I'd had more and more calls about situations like this one, and together we talked about a strategy for handling the young man's unacceptable behavior.

When I talk today with pastors and other leaders about youth ministry, I warn them to be ready to do more parenting than ever before. I say this because it's my experience that with more young people in single-parent homes and in homes where both parents are working, there is less time spent with parents, and some of the things we traditionally expected young people to know are simply not being taught. Further, young people are turning to a variety of adults for support and care. Often, that means a late night call to an advisor or church school teacher or youth ministry director from a teenager seeking help to deal with a problem or issue that used to be only in the parent's domain.

Covenant versus Contract

As you work with your group of young people, it is crucial that you are proactive in defining the behaviors that are expected in the group. Do this by creating a group covenant. Karen Akin, a pastor in Little Rock, Arkansas, provides this helpful difference between a covenant and a contract. Karen talks about agreeing with a young person in her youth group to pay him $20, and, in exchange, he agrees to mow her lawn. When he mows her lawn, she gives him $20. That's a *contract*—both sides have to keep their part of the agreement for it to work. A contract is conditional.

In contrast, when Karen makes a *covenant* with the young person to pay him $20, and he covenants with her to mow her lawn, even if he never mows her lawn, she still pays him $20. A covenant is not dependent on both sides doing what they promise. A covenant is only dependent on the promise itself. In a covenant, if the other party doesn't do his or her part, you aren't released from having to do your part. A covenant is unconditional. That's the miracle of the new covenant given to us through Jesus Christ. Even though we sin and fail over and over to keep our part of the covenant to be faithful to Christ, our salvation is still assured. God loves us still.

Creating a Covenant

Use the following process to create a covenant with your group.

1. First, using the illustration from Karen, explain the difference between a covenant and a contract. Then, explain that this covenant is needed so that group members have a common understanding of the behaviors that are expected when they are together.

2. If there are rules that are "givens," list these first. These should be few in number and primarily related to safety. For instance, "During youth group, if you must leave the building, first tell an adult leader," and so forth.

3. Now, post a blank sheet of newsprint and have a marker ready. Invite the group to state out loud any behavior they'd like to propose for the covenant to strengthen their life together as the body of Christ. When a suggestion is offered, thank the person and let the suggestion hover in the meeting area. Ask if there are any objections or questions about the suggestion. When you're trying for a consensus, ask the question "Can everyone live with that?" This question is different from whether or not you "like" something. If everyone can live with the covenant suggestion, write it up. Explain that once it's written, it is covenant for the group. As suggestions are being made, encourage those who make very specific suggestions to reword them to be broader. Look for phrases like "Encourage one another"; "Pray for one another"; "Avoid put-downs."

4. After you have written seven or eight items, end the covenant-building time and explain that you will revisit the covenant over the next few sessions. Invite group members to sign the covenant as a sign of their participation. Post the covenant in a prominent space. One youth group actually paints each year's covenant on the wall of their meeting area; then

everyone signs the wall with a marker. Visitors also sign when they come to the group.

5. During your life together, there will be times when the covenant is broken. When this happens, invite group members to call a "covenant check." Covenant checks are to be taken seriously. I tell groups that covenant checks are equivalent to pulling the red cable in the subway cars in New York City. When you pull that cable, you not only shut down that train, but also delay every train on that line. The same is true for a covenant check. Everything stops and the leader asks why that person called for the covenant check. As much as possible, the situation is resolved then and there, often in private away from the group. Warn that covenant checks should not be abused.

6. Over the next few sessions, revisit the covenant every time you meet so it becomes familiar to the group. This will help them remember the promise they've made. Remind them, too, that the covenant is not conditional. Just because someone else is not keeping his or her part of the covenant, it does not release others from having to keep their part.

Most groups who use the covenant process change covenants every year. Some change them every quarter. Groups with whom I've worked form a covenant once a year and then form specific covenants for lock-ins, mission trips, and so on. Even though you may have a covenant in place and the whole group understands what is expected, you may still have problems with the behavior of an individual.

Being a "Proactive" Leader

Good leaders know that being proactive rather than only reactive helps to head off potential problems in a group or classroom. For instance, in building a covenant, you've shared with everyone the common expectations for behavior. That's being proactive in managing the behavior of the group. What are some other ways of being proactive?

1. Use the covenant as the basis for complimenting and praising group members. If "Listen to one another" is on the covenant, then take a moment to say to group members that you really appreciated their listening to others. These positive words reinforce the behaviors hoped for and discourage the behaviors you want to avoid.

2. Keep the session flowing. It's a common understanding that when middle-schoolers get bored, they become destructive. Do your best to offer a "seamless" session where there is no significant time when they might get bored. For high-schoolers, you don't have to offer the same kind of schedule, but for early adolescents, it's the difference between an unruly and a pleasant group. Remember, even the ones who misbehave don't enjoy the group when they do.

3. Consider the meeting area and remove potential problems. If you know that a certain group member enjoys breaking crayons and tossing them at others, then put the crayons away. If you're sure that two members in the same small group will be a problem, then preassign groups so they're separated. Anticipate any problems, and do your best to head them off. That's the essence of being proactive!

But What Can I Do If There Is Still a Problem?

So you've faithfully built a covenant, and you're doing your best to be proactive, and you still have a problem with a group member or group members? It's important that young people know there are consequences for behavior that is not helpful for the body of Christ. If someone in the group is not behaving as he or she should, consider the following consequences. Envision these consequences as if they are each on a stairway with the top of the stairs being the most serious of consequences.

Step One: Ignore the Behavior

First, try to ignore what is happening. This first strategy requires the least work on your part. Classroom behavior management theory says that if you ignore the behavior and provide neither negative nor positive reinforcement, the behavior will eventually extinguish itself. How long should you ignore the behavior? It depends on the behavior. If someone's life is at immediate risk, obviously you should not ignore what is happening! But if there are two group members talking a little loudly, try ignoring the behavior first. Each person's tolerance level is different. Ignore it for as long as you can do so comfortably or until the behavior begins to distract the others. Then, move to the next step.

Step Two: The Look

Continue to glance at the individual or individuals who are the cause of the problem until they catch your eye. When they do, let them know you see them. A raised eyebrow. A steady stare. A nod of the head. Even a glare will communicate that the behavior needs to stop. For some young people, this will be too subtle to notice. If the behavior continues, move to step three.

Step Three: Physical Proximity

As you are leading, or, better yet, if you're one of the leaders who are free and the behavior is continuing, move yourself toward the individuals who are misbehaving. Make your way toward them and, if possible, stand or sit next to them. Your physical presence is often enough to extinguish the behavior.

Step Four: Physical Touch

If your presence is not enough, then gently place your hand on the young person's shoulder or arm in an appropriate touch. This is a light touch to show that you are there. Skilled teachers can move through all these steps smoothly and without breaks in instruction. If your physical presence and touch are not having any effect or if they only stop the behavior for a moment and then it continues, move on to the verbal cue.

Step Five: Verbal Cue

A verbal cue is a naming of the individuals and a direction. "Gus, please turn around and give me your attention." "Debra, have a seat right where you are and listen, please." Always make the verbal cue in the form of a request. Always use a polite tone. Avoid shouting or sounding angry. An edge to your voice is not a bad thing, but control by intimidation, threat, and power is not good behavior management. If the verbal cue is ineffective or if you have to give it more than once, give *one* warning, and only one. Say to the young person, "Mark, the next time I have to ask you to be quiet it will be outside of the room. Understand?" Get some kind of cue from Mark that he understands the consequence. If Mark still doesn't get it, then ask him to step outside. If you're the only adult leader in the group, ask the group for a time-out while you go and talk with Mark. If there are other leaders, ask them to take over while you talk with Mark.

Step Six: Time-Out

Step outside for conversation. Before you start talking, check yourself. If you're really angry, now is not the time. Count to ten backward and breathe slowly. When you're talking to the young person, get on his or her eye level. Don't lecture. Ask a series of questions:

You: Mark, what happened in there?

Mark: Nothing.

You: Well, why are you out here?

Mark: Because you told me to come out here.

You: And why did I do that?

Mark: I don't know.

You: Try to think of a reason. Why would I send you out here?

Mark: Because you hate me.

You: Mark, nothing could be further from the truth. I don't hate you. I love you.

(Mark mumbles under his breath something like "You have a stupid way of showing it." Wisely, you choose to ignore this comment.)

You: Come on, Mark. There is a good reason why you're out here. What is it?

Mark: Because I wouldn't stop talking and messing around with Josh.

You: You're right. Do you enjoy being out here?

Mark: It's not so bad.

You: Where would you rather be? Out here, or in there with the group?

Mark: In there with the group.

You: Okay. We're going to go back in and try it again. In order to avoid coming out here again, what do you have to do differently?

Mark: Not talk so much and not hit Josh.

You: And how might you best accomplish that?

Mark: What do you mean?

You: Fair question. I'm wondering if there are places you could sit other than beside Josh.

Mark: Okay. Forever?

You: No. But for the rest of class, yes.

Mark: Okay.

You: And, Mark, I do love you and Josh and everyone else in the class.

Mark: Yeah, whatever.

You: Let's go back in.

In this conversation, you are not lecturing. It's important that the young person understand what he or she did to end up outside the room having a talk like this. It's also important that the young person name behaviors to avoid being talked to like this again. You should do as little talking as possible. Take every comment seriously, but don't go overboard. For instance, Mark's little wisecrack about a "stupid way of showing it" was an adolescent attempt at goading you on. Remember, you're the adult! Don't fall for those little comments. Part of his developmental task now is to challenge authority, and he's just fulfilling his role. You fulfill yours as a loving, fair, and consistent leader.

Step Seven: Contact with Parents/Stepparents/Caregivers

The next step, if it comes to that, and in most cases it does not, is to contact the child's parents/stepparents/caregivers. For many young people, this is a huge deterrent. If you are at this place, start with a phone call and just check in with the parent/stepparent/caregiver. You need not even say there's a problem. Just ask how the individual is doing at home and what he or she says about church school or youth group. If you feel comfortable, bring up the concern over the phone. If not, a visit is probably best. Bring another adult leader with you. Don't make this something bigger than it is, but at the same time, don't diminish the problem.

Step Eight: Expulsion

The final step is to expel the individual from the program or classroom. This can be temporary or for the rest of the year. If you come to this place, there are serious behavior disorders here, and the parents/stepparents/caregivers need to be informed. Pastors and church educators must be involved in the conversation. Alternatives might be proposed, but remember, there are other young people and families involved.

I once had a long conversation with a parent who was distraught because the youth group had collapsed. One young person had bullied and intimidated all the other young people so that no one wanted to come to the youth group. The pastor and adult advisors refused to expel the young man even though he was always causing problems. I assured the parent that expelling an individual is a very real option and that at times God's grace can best be demonstrated through showing a young person that certain behavior is unacceptable and that there are consequences for being disruptive and disrespectful.

Prayer undergirds all of these consequences. Romans 8:26 reminds us that when we do not know how to pray, the Holy Spirit prays on our behalf. As you work through difficult and complex issues around managing behavior in a group, remember that the Holy Spirit is praying on your behalf even when you don't know how to pray!

Praise versus Encouragement

In their book *Positive Discipline in the Classroom: How to Effectively Use Class Meetings and Other Positive Discipline Strategies*, Jane Nelsen, Lynn Lott, and H. Stephen Glenn draw an important distinction between praise and encouragement. The authors are critical of the use of praise, because by its nature, praise only recognizes the best attempt or the completed, perfect product. In attaching our comments to a person's behavior ("I really like the way you're sitting quietly"), we teach that person that their self-worth comes from others' judgment of them and only when they perform accordingly. Encouragement, say the authors, recognizes effort and improvement, and because comments are attached to the nature of the person rather than to behavior ("I so appreciate your generous cooperation"), self-worth is based less on performance and more on who the person is. Try to affirm young people in the group with less praise tied to a specific behavior and more encouragement related to the person's whole being.

6
Small Youth Groups

I was the preacher for the day in one of our small rural churches in Maine. In the congregation that morning there were about thirty-five people. The church building consisted of the sanctuary and there was a small building next door with three meeting rooms. A few minutes into the service, we passed the peace of Christ to each other. The pastor and I left the chancel area to move among the people. I greeted five or six and then began to make my way back to my seat. When I was almost there, the pastor came over and said, "You might want to continue greeting people. This will take a while." He was right. We spent nearly twenty minutes passing the peace! As I talked with different members, I overheard others exchanging recipes, sharing news about their businesses, scheduling appointments for later in the week, talking about their health, and inquiring about children and grandchildren. Later I told the pastor I had not been to a worship service where the passing of the peace was more essential than the preaching of the Word. He laughed and explained that while they were eager to hear the Word, the passing of the peace was important, too.

That's one of the joys of the small-membership church. People can really know each other. On that Sunday morning, most of the folks in the congregation could name everyone else in the sanctuary and probably give a lengthy history on each person. But does that mean everything is better in a small-membership congregation? No. There are struggles there just as there are struggles in medium- and large-membership churches. In fact, there is some evidence that young people in smaller congregations are somewhat neglected. That finding is just the opposite of what I would have expected. Look at the results of a survey taken by the Barna Research Group in Southern California. They surveyed young people in small (under 150 members), medium (150–500 members), and large (more than 500 members) congregations, and what they found was startling.

The percentages listed below reflect the number of youth who "agree strongly" with each statement.

1. Jesus Christ rose from the dead and reappeared on earth after his resurrection.

    Small: 55%

    Medium: 74%

    Large: 85%

2. There is a personal God who watches over us and can be reached by our prayers.

    Small: 59%

    Medium: 77%

    Large: 67%

3. Jesus Christ is alive today.

    Small: 34%

    Medium: 51%

    Large: 62%

4. The Christian church is relevant for today.

    Small: 38%

    Medium: 43%

    Large: 44%

5. There is no spiritual force that rules the universe. We are totally in control of our own lives.

    Small: 16%

    Medium: 13%

    Large: 5%

---

*"Crisis in Small Churches," *Group Magazine* (September 1991): 36. Reprinted with permission from *Group Magazine*, copyright © 1991, Group Publishing, Box 481, Loveland CO 80539.

The results in this survey were startling because it was thought that the small-membership church was *more* likely to communicate the truths of the gospel than the large-membership church, where young people were more likely to get lost. Instead, what the researchers found was that in small-membership congregations, where there might be only one or two teenagers, everyone assumed the young people were included. Everyone assumed they were hearing the gospel message because, after all, they had been in church all their lives and everyone knew them. In contrast, in large-membership congregations, because they were afraid of losing contact with the many young people, a staff person was hired whose singular task was to be in ministry with the young people and their families. Young people actually received more attention in large-membership churches with one hundred and fifty young people on the membership rolls than in smaller churches with three young people.

Hurdles of Small Youth Groups

If your congregation includes a handful of young people, there are no doubt hurdles that you face.

1. Lack of time and attention to young people.

The truth is that when there are fewer people around, people have more to do. Many leadership needs are identical for small-, medium-, and large-membership churches. The work grows exponentially, but the tasks are essentially the same. When there are fewer people, chances are you'll have a more difficult time recruiting leaders to teach church school or work with young people.

2. Sparse schedule of activities for youth.

Fewer people lead to fewer activities and that simply isn't as fun for the young people. The "fun quotient" in youth ministry is an important one, and it's hard to compete with full-blown youth programs that have activities happening every week.

3. Few finances.

With fewer people come fewer dollars. Spread the cost of a mission trip among thirty-five people and it's less than the same trip for three.

4. Critical mass needed for fun.

A lot of the activities suggested call for at least a small group of eight to ten. If you have a group of three or four, it can be difficult to adapt the curriculum. And with young people, there is such a thing as a critical mass. It seems to take at least eight to ten to get a sense of the group.

5. Sibling challenges.

Often in a small-membership church with three or four youth, you have a combination of siblings because to pull them all together, you need to broaden the age range. This can be a problem when siblings are tired of being with each other or are in the midst of an argument or a fight.

Strengths of Small Youth Groups

While there are probably other hurdles you can name, it's important that we recognize the strengths of a small youth group. There are many. I've listed here a few that I've experienced.

Intimacy

Fewer numbers simply mean that you are more apt to know more about each other, and the more you know, the more you are apt to be involved in each others' lives. Further, small-membership congregations are less likely to be as transient as large-membership congregations. Therefore, people share a history with each other that grows over the years. All of this leads to a depth and intimacy that only can be found by forming small groups in medium and large congregations. When members of small congregations have been asked what they cherish most about their church, they often say something about how they know everyone and everyone knows them. But beyond the knowing is a sense of caring.

One young family had just joined a small church, and within a year, the mother was diagnosed with cancer. Throughout almost two years of hospital visits and chemotherapy, the members of that small congregation delivered a dinner meal every day. A host of adopted grandparents babysat the young children for countless hours, as the father spent nights at the hospital with his wife. At the end of those two years, in full remission from the cancer and recovering from the rigorous therapies, the mother said, "I don't care what happens; I am never leaving this church. This church saved my family and me through their prayers and through their actions. I am never leaving this church." That's what intimacy is.

Community Is Family

While it can feel confining to some, the whole community of the church becomes family for these young people. One young person told me that, while growing up in a small church in Montana, he had so many multiple mothers and fathers that "I couldn't get away with nothing. I'd be running through the hall chasing after somebody and an adult would come around the corner and yell my first, middle, and last name, and I'd quit whatever trouble I was making. And that adult wasn't even related to me! Nearly drove me crazy!" Growing up in a small-membership church gives a sense of community as family. That adult knew his first, middle, and last name because he probably had seen him baptized as an infant and had grown up with him. It's part of what being family means.

Opportunities for Leader Development

With fewer people, the congregation is more likely to turn to young people for leadership. In fact, regarding the issue of integration, we have many small-membership churches who have a young person on session because they watched that young person grow up, and they trust his or her knowledge and commitment. Besides that, with so few members, young people are needed. When it was one small Oklahoma congregation's turn to send an elder commissioner to the General Assembly, they elected an elder who was seventeen years old. "He was the best qualified," the session clerk told me over the phone. "He keeps us old folks on session on our toes." It was amusing. That year, the youth advisory delegate from that presbytery was older than one of the commissioners!

Flexibility

I was with one of our pastors in a small church in rural Idaho. He wasn't sure how many young people were going to come to the special meeting that had been called to talk with me. When we got to the church, we found two young people there waiting. Eventually a third came. The pastor was pleased because there were six young people possible, and he was hoping for two.

Rather than sit at the church building, we walked together down to a local cafe and sat down at a table. We shared hot chocolate and talked and laughed. I modified the group-building activity I had planned, and then we discussed the "Top 10 questions of faith." We looked up passages in the Bibles we had brought with us and closed in prayer. It was a wonderful time—relaxed and informal. That's the kind of gift small groups bring. With a group of five, we can wander into a restaurant and talk together without calling ahead to make reservations and figuring out transportation needs. Truly, it's a gift.

Identity

One of the key developmental tasks for adolescents is to form their identity. Often, young people in small-membership churches have a head start on this because they know others in the congregation and are known by them. Young people know their baptism stories because adults in their congregation have told them over and over. Young people know the stories of the church because adults tell them. All this helps to form the identity that is crucial for young people.

A Word about a Program Model

Carol Seaton, a General Assembly staff colleague who has pastored a small-membership congregation in West Virginia and works with small churches, has often told me that if she could do anything, it would be to give each small-membership church a "self-esteem pill." "They would take that pill and then stop comparing themselves to large churches. They would stop using their small size as an excuse!" she said. I think Carol is onto something. Our whole culture is consumed by numbers and size. Bigger is not always better. If you are a small-membership congregation with a few young people, there is no need for you to try and duplicate a model of a one-thousand-member congregation with a full-time youth ministry director and one hundred and fifty adolescents in the program with eight adult advisors and four church school teachers!

There is nothing in the Bible that says you have to meet as a youth group once a week. I tell small-membership congregations to gather their young people at least once a quarter for an overnight. Go somewhere and use a good curriculum for study and group building through the weekend. Then take the group to a large conference in the summer and do some kind of mission work perhaps linked with the presbytery or another group to increase your numbers. Finally, be sure to integrate your young people into the whole church. This is one of the many gifts that small-membership congregations offer to young people—the opportunity to be a part of the church rather than some separate program.

Ten Strategies for Working with a Small Youth Group

To continue, I offer the following ten strategies for working with a small youth group.

1. Keep a positive attitude. Accentuate the positive. Too often, small youth groups develop a poor self-image because they're told they're too small to matter. Value those who are there. Appreciate the participation genuinely. Make each person feel important and welcome. Leaders with positive attitudes help keep morale high.

2. Do long-range planning. Long-range planning is just as valuable in small groups as in large groups. It communicates that the group has direction and stability. You can count on the group doing something worthwhile in the future. Long-range planning also establishes and values traditions and rituals.

3. *Avoid competing with the megachurch mentality.* You need not do the same kinds of activities as a large group. Set realistic goals for yourself. Do your best not to feel threatened.

4. *Never cancel an activity because of low attendance.* If you cancel an event because of low attendance, you risk communicating to those who did attend that they're not worth your time. Be thankful for those who did come, be flexible, and enjoy yourselves.

5. *Meet in an appropriate space.* Room dynamics can dramatically affect the spirit, tone, and climate of a group. Choose a space that is slightly larger than needed. Do all you can to make the space comfortable and positive.

6. *Combine with other groups.* Establish an ongoing relationship with another similar-sized group. Plan a few events together during the year.

7. *Participate in presbytery, synod, General Assembly, and other events.* It is valuable for young people to see they really are *not* alone. There are others who are, like them, faithful. Other events include concerts and theme parks. All these types of large events will help satisfy the need for connection with others.

8. *Include young people in the whole life of the church.* A small group cannot provide all the young people with all the challenges they need to grow as faithful disciples of Jesus Christ. Involve young people in other aspects of the church's life. Since you can't have a youth music program, direct young people who want to sing to participate in the adult choir, for instance.

9. *Value age differences.* Although you may only have a handful of young people, there are simply too many developmental differences to group them together for too long. Value the differences in ages. Structure a variety of activities and be creative in age groupings.

10. *Develop mentor relationships.* Pair young people and adults in the congregation in mentor relationships. Provide a list of activities for the clusters to do. Meet with the mentors to help

them understand what you're hoping will happen. Monitor the progress of the mentor groups.

I hope these suggestions have been helpful as you look at your youth ministry program. It's easy to get discouraged in a culture that equates higher numbers with success and even faithfulness! Whenever you are down, take time to read Judges 7 about Gideon, and remember that our God is able to do mighty things with only a few!

Bibliography

Chromey, Rick. *Youth Ministry in Small Churches*. Loveland, CO: Group Publishing, 1990.

Cummings, Carol. *Teaching Makes a Difference*, 2nd ed. Edmonds, WA: Teaching, Inc., 1990.

Elkind, David. *All Grown Up and No Place to Go: Teenagers in Crisis*. Reading, MA: Addison-Wesley Publishing Co., 1984.

Fowler, James W. *Stages of Faith: The Psychology of Human Development and the Quest for Meaning*. San Francisco: HarperSanFrancisco, 1981.

Nelsen, Jane, Lynn Lott, and H. Stephen Glenn. *Positive Discipline in the Classroom: How to Effectively Use Class Meetings and Other Positive Discipline Strategies*. Rocklin, CA: Prima Press, 1993.

Rice, Wayne. *Great Ideas for Small Youth Groups*. Grand Rapids, MI: Zondervan, 1986.

Turnage, Lynn. *Surveying the Land*. Louisville, KY: Bridge Resources, 1997.

Westerhoff, John H. *Will Our Children Have Faith*? San Francisco: HarperSanFrancisco, 1983.

White, Vera K. *Youth in Peacemaking*. Louisville, KY: Presbyterian Peacemaking Program, 1992. DMS order #259-92-917. Call (800) 524-2612.

About the Writer

Rodger Nishioka is the coordinator for youth and young adult ministries in the Christian Education program area of the General Assembly Council of the Presbyterian Church (U.S.A.). An elder at the Church of Christ Presbyterian in Park Ridge, Illinois, Rodger also is a full-time student at McCormick Theological Seminary in Chicago. He is studying for a master of arts in theological studies and plans to pursue a Ph.D. in religious education. Rodger served as the Associate for Youth Ministry with the General Assembly and taught English and social studies at Curtis Jr. High School in Tacoma, Washington. Rodger enjoys being outdoors, visiting the beach, and eating sushi.